the RINGMASTER'S ARRAY

BILL HARRIS

PAST TENTS PRESS

Plays by Bill Harris

Queen of Sheba
Riffs
Robert Johnson: Trick the Devil
Coda
Every Goodbye Ain't Gone
Stories About the Old Days
Up and Gone Again
The Society of Men
Slave Narrative
He Who Endures
The Dog on the Victrola
Warn the Wicked
No Use Crying

the RINGMASTER'S ARRAY

impressions by

Bill Harris

inspired by

the photographs of Roy DeCarava
the collages of Romare Bearden
the music of Duke Ellington

Published by Past Tents Press
332 W. Woodland, Ferndale, MI 48220

Cover Design by Paul Schwarz

Distributed by Small Press Distribution
1341 Seventh Street, Berkeley, CA 94710

Printed by Cushing-Malloy, Inc.
1350 N. Main St., Ann Arbor, MI 48107

Copyright© 1997 Bill Harris
Cover Art: "Miles Away" *36x36 in.* Carole Harris, 1991
Bio Photograph by Bill Sanders

Library of Congress Card Catalogue Number : 97-67586
ISBN: 0-9622474-7-2

Table of Contents

On the Music of Duke Ellington

for Carole

On the Photographs of
Roy DeCarava

*Based on "**Roy DeCarava: A Retrospective**," Museum of Modern Art, N.Y., NY, 1996 and "**The Sound I Saw**," Studio Museum of Harlem, N.Y., NY, 1983*

Film Noir

for Roy DeCarava

Picture him:
in some soot-
black setting.

Eye
like a miner's lamp.

Tone & Substance

for Roy DeCarava

I. Tone

Grey
veils the frame like gauze;
like times tough as flint; like
mirror backs or meditation; like
layers of ash over yesterday.

The eye
must adjust, must work
for the reward of subtleties
swaddled in shadows
and reluctantly revealed.

2. Substance

Illuminator. Captor
of the reverent common,
of the grey nuances that linger
like a once known melody;
like the way your mama called your name—

the dim detail. So second nature
it has faded to a faint hum
on the lip of the brain. But,
is the exact, the exacting detail:

pomade waves in the hornman's hair
glimpse of French cuff,
glint on the instrument's bell, tilt
of the singer's head, the finger's curl;

the unconscious gesture, as familiar
as prenatal memories connected to cowries
and creek baptisms, reflecting our genealogy,
demanding recognition and acknowledgment
and celebration.

That makes you whisper, Yes!
As you bear witness
to these beshadowed testaments.

Makes you nod your head,
nod your head and pat your foot...
Makes you say A-
men. And again, Amen.

Coltrane, Half Note, New York, 1960

Man. Musician. Not a saint or martyr.
His life's late Call: Repent. Revere. Reveal
to those who'd hear. Roil the mainstream's water.
Probe what the unfathomed might conceal
unrelentingly, with a convert's zeal.

Trane purged, purified himself, then began
with a screamsound, as pure as thunderpeal
bursting unbound, antediluvian,
to bring light to the murk of Stygian
gloom; express wonder at the sensed, the seen;
to give beauty — like fire — Promethean;
to be in awe; be sanctified — serene.

Sought light midst dark. Bore witness with paean
psalms glorifying grey-truths protean.

Coltrane and Ben Webster, New York, 1960

Where most take baby steps, (if
there's movement at
all) Ben
strode in titan boots,
brute stepping
while toting the usual burden-
some business...

all the while, without
subjection or contradiction,

producing preachments
in a breath of roaring fire
and wee small hours whisperings;
his own school.

And Trane,
envious and loving
(without subjection or contradiction), goes,
like a thunder-frightened child
to the heat source, the
heart, embraces
for all
he is worth.

Coltrane and Elvin, New York, 1960

Elvin, dark
metamorphic
moon hovers,
      jack-o'-lanternlike,
      like the wraith
      of the legion of
      ancestral drummers,
      their thundering rhythm-
      waves resounding all-
      the-way-back, all-the-way-
      back beyond before, all-
      the-way-back over
      time and over seas,
      and Elvin oversees
          and backs the changes... And John,
          focused,
          in the foreground,
          (on the edge and
          mindless of the dangers
          of course) on course;
calling forth the host by means of his golden mettle.

Coltrane Alone #4a, New York, 1963

Interior: night:
on the stand.
Prior to the first set.
Tenor in hand.

Silence, (save
for the shutter's wink).
Seeking strength and will
for the continuing pursuit.

Will I "perform," be
this evening's entertainment,
attendant
to table-talk and tippling, or
will I ride the leap and throb
of Elvin, Jimmy and McCoy's pulse,

and through chance and changes
rise (past finger-popping
and the limits of execution) to
intuition; will

the breath and being of my call
converge, ignite, convert sound
to Light, and
enkindle the assembled; trans-

forming this Lascaux-like cavern,
with its obsidian whispers, into a haven
secure from the measure
and canons of day's light?

Billie and Hazel at Party, New York, 1957

a party.
lamp lit. relaxed.

no tears
no blues. no regret
no grief on this set.

laughs. yes. joy,
in the being,
the moment.

not the lady
of the tabloids, the blotter.
just Hazel Scott's buddy,
Clarence's kid.
Pres' ace:

    Billie

Billie, New York, 1952

(Was always herself
she gave us. We
only reciprocated
when we

wanted.)

Broke feeling down
word by word.

Turned blues
into every hue, shade and value.
Floated them on a tongue kiss breeze
licking across the wilted gardenia
of our notion of love.

Wasn't never no place
to warm herself, except
the cold sweat-stained,
torn at the seams white silk dues
of dope.

The mystery
is how she lasted long as she did,
life being such a persistent bitch,
and we doing all we could
to help her do away with herself.

Basie and Lena, New York, 1957

haiku

1.
Redbank's Bill Basie
grinning, like he is being
hugged by Lena Horne.

2.
With Lena hugging,
Redbank's Bill Count Basie beams.
I would. You would too.

3.
Pretty Lena in
her turban. Mr. Basie
in his tie. My, my.

4.
Beauty and the Beat.
Plink, plink. Tickled pink? Plink, plink.
One-mo'-time! Plink, plink.

Dancers, New York, 1956

Silhouette boogie men,
anonymous embodiers
of joys and rituals
as ancient as us,
combust
in semi-darkness,
shimmering like heat
off flames, like
spirits from our dark-
fantastic other world;
conjuring memories
of a million sundancers—
before and beyond.

Couple Dancing, New York, 1956

1.
Workdays she's *their*
girl. Is pleasant. Doesn't sass
or steal; the children
love her. (I'm
steady too.
Sober. Reliable. A
good one.)

Weekend ballads and embraces
are balms against the half-
light presumptions of
the Ma'ams and Masters
of our daily bread.

Must be their needful reflex,
caused by the swellelegant
dazzle from their gilt and means,
that insists on notions
of our devotion, our
humblehood; yet

is a luster
so limp
it fails to illuminate
beyond the pale.

Otherwise they couldn't look
the other way; not
see, fathom, and celebrate
for instance,
her determined carriage,
the astonishing insistence
of her posterior's extraordinary curve,

a sight so worthy of homage
it shades the sunshine of their
conquests, canvasses, notes,
lines, spires, creeds, philanthropies, and laws.

2.
Snug; each other's,
we move to the music, we
breathe in and out. We

pity the fools...

Milt Jackson, New York, 1956

Gray Gabriel blows

and Bags waits;

looking
for all the world
like some pinstriped pastor; some
messenger-reverend
in his glowing white shirt;

waits,
stele straight,
hands clasped,
chin up, head
cocked
as if to catch sight,
through the membrane of this swarth,
of the memory-flame
of men back home named boy;
with earthburns
in the creases of their calloused hands;

the memory
of rough-plank churches, jukes and barbershops;
the taste
of well water and lightnin' and bile
from swallowed gorge and bitten tongues;
droughts and floods
and moonlight and northbound trains and
rented rooms and blind pigs and storefronts;

Bags
waits

to bring that light
to his blues.

Booker Ervin and Listener, New York, 1961

Blow, Booker. Blow
your tough
tenor blues
with its Texas tinge, and tone
big as the
excess of the West;

all the while
hip

that behind you,
ceding neither
foot tap
nor fingersnap,

the man in the black suit,
reviewer
with the final word,

web weaver of scurvy snares
deep
    and dark
as your blues
       in the night.

Coleman Hawkins, Backstage,
Ellenville, N.Y., 1956

"That's what music is about...
The adventure..."

...the almost
casual
way
Hawk turned from America,

as he'd turn while soloing
to signal his pianist; or
while humming along with some
string quartet on the turntable, or
turn to turn
up or down the flame
under a pot of beans. Ex-

patriate
as easy as
running a scale;

shucked America

like charred husks from ears
of roasted Kansas corn...

Errol Garner, Joe Benjamin, Ellenville, N.Y., 1956

Had
(from the age of 3)
an orchestra in his fingertips.
Like having flowers
for thoughts.

Could,
on command,
and with elfin delight,
pull rabbits, doves and endless silks
from his reverie's sleeve; could

conjure the pomp and romp
of a circus parade.

In his left hand,
the rumble and stride
of the pachyderm's trudge
behind tamers of lions and throwers of knives
and walkers on stilts, high-wire, and rope;

and in his right,
more of the ringmaster's array:
show girls in net hose and fabulous feathers;
highflyers; bareback riders; the band;
teetering jugglers on single-wheeled cycles;
and a jumbling, bumbling babel of clowns
tumbling and stumbling
from a bantam sedan.

Monk at Piano, New York, 1955

Wee see Liza, Ruby and Lulu
rootie tooted
back to town.

Found Monk at piano,
and not. Got very Near Blue
'bout what was on his mind. *And
where was his chapeau,
at the Baroness' château?*

Evidence was
he was looking
another way. Split
lickety quick (without
so much as a Bye Ya), implying
it was on us now,
seeing as how he made his point
far back as '41.

Need he say
more?

Who know?

Duke Ellington, New York, 1967

You got it. Down. On
and between the lines.

Riffs
and rhapsodies.
Storefront
to Abyssinian. Jungle to
Sugar Hill.
All. Right
from the hip. Square business.
Quick cutters. Sharp as tacks.
Nailed in their tracks.

Harlem ought to be
writing you suites.

Johnny Hodges, New York, 1954

Forehead in his right hand
sits at the music stand
listening to the playback,
horn across his knees
like a sated, belly down babe.

Did —
did Duke's disciple —
what he is disciplined
to do; does
session after session. Night
after night. Blew
with his impassive
impassioned finesse,
a blue ballad,
deep-felt.

Yes. Did. Yet,
hearing, hears. Here. Now,
forehead in his right hand,
knows; as any with ears will:

a pure thing
purely done,

they'll sigh;

with the impact
of a throb of love
at the sight of some
lovesome thing.

And as its maker,
is put in mind of the reason
beyond the reason, and

is moved.

Ellington #9, Session Break, New York, 1954

...back to back
across the breach of our solitude
we wait, at this odd hour,
like wallflowers,
like empty coats.

Break over
we'll return
by ragged, rankless ones and twos;
a thesaurus of men,
petulant as schoolboys robbed of recess.

And he,
the Governor, the Maestro, the Old Man,
feigning indifference,
will prod us through our paces:

rehearsing morsels and scrawls
scribbled and dashed on fragments and scraps,

while slyly reminding us
of doodling or noodling bits
we blew
while warming up or cooling down,
"Let's keep that
in," he'll coo,
cool, playing us like puppets,

and we, competitive
and anxious to please,
give our individual bests.

Before we know it
we're
a band of men,
again.

On the Collages of Romare Bearden

Suite for Reclining Nudes
(a cycle of 5 poems
after the collages of
Romare Bearden)

Electric Evening

1.
She lies—dark in the
brightness of the sun—as open
as the river's mouth.

"Gal, you a river
hipped mama, n I swear I
come to be baptized."

Puts his arms around
her like a ring around the
blazing evening sun.

"You sweet n ripe like
melons in the good ol plump and
juicy summer time."

2.
       Was this what love was?
       Her easy rider; thoughts that
       smolder words that burn?

       Was it only to
       have but not to hold or to
       hold but not to have?

3.
Starts a-shovelin on the coal,
buildin up a head of steam;
"…don't sputter on me now,
yo locomotions a natchul dream.

Keep on the way you doin,
we ridin on the proper track.
I'm in a rumblin rollin frenzy."
Starts in to seethe n simmer,
like a spark in her tinderbox;
start in to heave n tremor;
hot enough to roast an ox.

4.
She lies — dark in moon's
brightness — opened as black clouds
in a driving rain.

      Was that all love was?
      Some sweet sweaty moments be-
      neath the setting sun?

      Not have or hold just
      the rumble and roll, the stuff
      of smoldering dreams?

Reclining Nude

She lies, naked, twisted
as the bedclothes,
her rambling, easy riding papa
done flagged that sundown train.

It's repeated, it's repeated
just like a blues refrain.

Alone to do her rocking
in the cold back
rocking chair.
Left her
and his guitar,
took and rode on away from there.

She lies empty
as a cup full of moonlight,
her coal-black, jelly rolling papa
done flagged that Northbound train.

It's repeated, it's repeated
just like a blues refrain.

Two Moons of Luvernia

(O, her dreams rise,
as her blues come down)

O, her dreams rise,
rise like the moon,
like a conjuring
Holy Ghost. Bewitching,
ripe-round. Eyeballer
of a thousand thousand
boardings, a thousand
thousand forced goodbyes.

O, her dreams rise,
rise, as her blues
come down,
come down like tears,
turning her blue-black cheeks
cherry red, come down
like the dark trickle of her
monthly blood, come
down like a cloudburst
of late spring rain.

O, her dreams rise,
rise as Luvernia lies,
her back turned to the wall,
reflected in her looking glass;
with the moon, a ball,
luminous lead, hanging
'bove her rumpled,
unpartnered bed.

O, her dreams rise,
rise and fill her place,
pine box plain,
window shuttered
'gainst the landscape
with the mind wrecking,
leave-taking train.

O, her dreams rise,
rise like the moon, who
knows about her blues;
has witnessed a thousand
thousand comings
and goings, but stares
cold—even in the hottest
night—silent as its
reflection.

O, her dreams rise,
as her blues come down,
and Luvernia knows,
even in her dreams
there'll never be enough,
never be enough light,
even from two full
moons, to bleach
her blues away.

O, her dreams rise,
as her blues come down.

Dream Images

No Lawd,
the dream don't come straight,
not in no half empty bed;
nor regular, like the rails,
but tangled, like the Hidden
Valley of her loins, twisted
as her bedclothes;
as her worried heart.

The dream of her
sweet cruel daddy—
who packed his bag
and took his leave—
comes, like moonlit silverbacked
reflections on the wall.
Broken, fleeting, like
his word, his love.

The lower, the locomotive
limbs—that he used to walk
the rutted road and 2-laned
blacktop to the junction—
ain't even in the dream.
And one arm, used to flag
that fleeting freight,
is missing, too.
Ain't it funny how dreams do.

But the body part
of her departed papa
pig iron hard and black,
is there, Yes Lawd. But
is broke off, separate
from the sweet talking,
love pledging part. Ain't
it funny how dreams be.

No Lawd,
a troubled dream
don't come whole,
nor rounded
like a full phase moon,
don't even come pieced,
patterned like patchwork.

A troubled dream
be's torn asunder,

Yes Lawd,
with parts lopped off.

Sunset Limited

How Long How Long...?

Holding the unhad babe she stands before herself in the thicket where she lies, cold ground for her bed; dreaming still: the stud-stallion sups; rooster, coop sovereign, struts.

*—Made me love
you, now your train done come...*

And the bird, black as the longest night, circles, echoing the Limited's long gone whistle—which goose pimples, even in the hottest night—as it mocks and rocks toward Ol' Hannah, who uncaring, puts day to death; continuing, even in her dreams, to fall, and rise. And fall and rise.

How long How long...?

She feels, even in her dream, the roll and rumble, the arrival, the pulling out, the moving up the line.

Dreaming still, and yet, even in her dream, they pay no mind; fall, rise, sup, strut, they go on, as she, too, on waking, must.

—Made me love you, now your train done gone....

Patchwork Quilt

for Carole

Coal-black and She-ba comely,
head wrapped 'round in rags,
she lies alone in naked memory;
patch of pubic brier
'gainst her hotchedpotched handiwork.

    The motley patterns—
defying the rules
of the ruling aesthetic—
      please; send the eye
a-romp, like Saturday nighters
      to the fiddler's reel.

Coal-black and She-ba comely,
tar Baby of Tradition,
she lies alone on the patchworked
remnants of her life.

On the Jazz of
Duke Ellington

The Queen's Suite
New Orleans Suite

The Queen's Suite

The six movements represent the "beauty experiences" of Duke Ellington's life. Written for Queen Elizabeth II. (haiku)

1. Sunset and the Mockingbird

Autumn sunset's rays
rise, like the riffed trills of an
unseen mockingbird.

2. Lightning Bugs and Frogs

Moonlit frogs; choral
croakers accompanying the
lightning bug's ballet.

3. Northern Lights

The Northern Lights: Earth's
Halo—evidence of the
majesty of God.

4. Le Sucrier Velours[†]

Le Sucrier Velours
sings songs sugar sweet —*l'image*
même de la beauté.

[†] the Soft, Sweet Singing Bird

5. Apes and Peacocks

Thought: Midst gifts most grand —
to Solomon from She-Ba—
the peacocks and ape!

6. The Single Petal of a Rose

Duke plays—as from the
rose, a single petal falls...
Beauty of beauties...

New Orleans Suite

*Duke's homage to the
birthplace of jazz, in five
movements and four portraits*

Blues for New Orleans

Ran into Buddy Bolden
on Rampart and Perdido,
as'ed him
'bout his sound.

And Buddy Bolden say,
"Got some taboo Congo Square
tongue-chanting
and possession dancing to the *grand tambour's*
pound pound pound,
in my sound,"
Buddy Bolden say.

And Buddy Bolden say,
"Got some blind singers
hollering 'bout women,
weather or whitefolks done
dogged 'em down
to the ground,
in my sound,"
Buddy Bolden say.

And Buddy Bolden say,
"Got some street peddler bellowing
'bout 'Flowers, fruit, and fish,
freshest can be found!'
in my sound,"
Buddy Bolden say.

And Buddy Bolden say,
"Got some roustabout heave an' hos
hollered from docks and levees
and there around
in my sound,"
Buddy Bolden say.

And Buddy Bolden say,
"Got some second line shouting
when brass bands cut a strut
to send the departed
ramblin' on, heaven or hellbound,
in my sound,"
Buddy Bolden say.

And Buddy Bolden say,
"Got some funky butt
mattress back whore hollers
from way back o' town,
trying to 'tract
some Saturday night smuthound
to lay his money down,
in my sound,"
Buddy Bolden say.

And Buddy Bolden say,
"Got some old and young sisters
Sunday morning amening and swaying
to the preacher's praying
'bout Jesus, their joy and crown,
in my sound,"
Buddy Bolden say.

Bourbon Street Jingling Jollies

1.
She sits, slack legged,
in singlet and snagged black hose.

The daybreak breeze
stirs the alley-view window's lace,
the delicate first light
yellows the still life
of her bureau, her
chipped pitcher and basin, her
pot, and her crib's peeling
rose patterned walls.

Memories maneuver
through the rising rays
like shadow puppets grind-
dancing to a funky-butt tune
with a Spanish tinge.

2. "Whush a gal like you..!?"
     one of last night's sailors,
     who loved that thing, laughed
     and lurched and lurched and laughed,
     too juiced to solve the buttons
     on his bell-bottom's fly.

3.   "What's, *A gal like me?'!*"

4.   In her professional passion
         in the pastel wash
         of her silk draped lamp
         she'd undone him, pulled
         him into place, snarled
         above the creak and groan
         "Oh, jazz me, daddy! Jazz your
         jingling jolly, your Blue Book,
         Bourbon Street bawd!"

5.   "*'A gal like me...'*

         I just be doing what I know.
         And I know what I be doing
         when I be doing it. God
         damn!"

Thanks for the Beautiful Land of the Delta

The crescent city.
Cradled in the delta
of the big river's bend—

En bas du Vieux Carré,
the colored resort,
Spanish Fort, on
as sweet a Sunday
as the Lord's ever sent.

Giving his battered cornet's keys
a jittery finger-tap in martial time,
he watches the colored
and Creole *gens de couleur*
the *crème de la crème*
assembling for their pic-nics
and concert by his
GOLDEN LIBERTY BRASS BAND.

No barrel house here,
nor bucking,
none of that
low, District jazz
or jive or creep-joint funky-butt.

We're not like bar rats
ragging time
from brothel
to bordello
and back again. No. Not
Hot, liquored, bowlderized, but
legitimate, orthodox. Like

—magnolias
in the afternoon—like
priests,
in the pulpit of the park.

This glorious day
me and my musicians
play for the settled;
Society;

the aristocrats
of New Orleans.

Portrait of Louis Armstrong

Okeh recording studio,
Chicago, 28 June, 1928.

King Oliver's Little Louie,
Dippermouth, Satchmo,

could only have bubbled up
out of that Delta gumbo
of Vieux Carré,
Tenderloin, and Garden District conflicts:

complexion, place, creed, and politics;

seasoned with Back o' Town's pastiche
of deprivation and parades
and ragtime pimps with gold teeth,
tippin' 'round razor toting whores
with treasonous dreams.

Savoring the gage's last sweet drag,
Louie rasps, "Call to order, gates,
we here to make some music,
so let's do that thing.
How 'bout *West End Blues,*
a-one..."

and his flashing cadenza
cascades from the bell
like a thundering from the Lord,
downflowing
onto the old river's deep waters,

overswelling its banks and levees,

and henceforth and forever
rerouting the mighty mainstream's course.

Portrait of Sidney Bechet

First filled Duke's ears
in D.C. 'round '21.
"Greatest thing I ever heard,"
lauded the Master, and
taking one to know one,
labeled the roly-poly
New Orleans native "an
original," and "truly great."

And Bechet,
as articulate
with reed as word,
telling his tale from gut and loin,
Nouvelle Orléans au naturel, straight
as his horn.

It was
what it was:
a way to forget; a
means to remember; a
livelihood; not intellectual
or aesthetic, it was
a scuffle: a satchel,
some rotgut liquor
in some cutthroat
cabarets. Socks
washed in a cold water sink.

                    (Creole
of color, adored on the Continent,
for reasons of their own.)
                    It was
a joy some-
times. Sometimes
not.
      In the face of it
I played my ragtime, when,
where I could.

What else
was there to do?

Second Line

"That's the life!"
thought the boy,
scuffing up dust and dreaming
as he danced along beside.

"I'm go'n' get out
these knickers!
Get in the world of cribs
and spats.
      An' when
I be tonking, or play pic-nics,
burial or parades
go'n' toot 'em to me
from far as West End,
Bucktown 'n' Spanish Fort.

          (Then
they won't bother 'bout me being "coal
complected, with hair like cockleburs.")

An' when my time be over
and they tote me to my final rest,
the mens'll say, 'Did'n 'e ramble.'
An' the womens'll holler,
'Did'n 'e
buck an' jazz, Lord,
did'n 'e buck
an' jazz!'"

Portrait of Wellman Braud

bassist with Duke Ellington Orchestra 1926 -1935

Wellman, impatient,
pats his foot as blood-metric
       and in tempo as the
pump-pumping wheel-rail
       repetition; the steady
surge and sway
       of the southbound
Crescent City Special.
       Next
stop,
       New
Orleans.

       We — cool cats all, we rock
in this Pullman, rented to outfox
ol' Jim Crow — we laze like well fed felines,
while Duke jots with lines and dots.

       I squint through night-black
and time for first sight
of home: glorious city of culinary,
musical and earthly delights.

       At the Cotton Club
we amused mobsters, were
Exotica for the Caucasian
Café Society set.

But, overseas
we are renowned.
Full men. We
receive royalty.
We reign.

The whistle sings out—
clear as a Creole Love Call,
seductive as Buddy
Bolden's beckoning wail—
Next stop
New Orleans.

Aristocracy à la Jean LaFitte

Jean LaFitte,
(1780?-1825?)
Cajun privateer,
whose unheralded participation
during the siege of New Orleans
saved the colony's fat
from Britain's fire. And,

Duke, (1899-1974). Each

his own
man,

and, a leader

of men,
of bands of men.

Sailed hostile seas
under colors of grandeur,
elegance, grace;

wielding style
like foils,
to oppose an armada of contempt
for the offense of self-possessed,
unrepentant

otherness.

Portrait of Mahalia Jackson

Mahalia,
mammy bosomed Lord praiser;
chicken frying, rafter shaker.

Knew
whereof she sang
when she shouted Christ's
burning and shining light
on ol' Satan,
exposing his low-down tempting ways.

Mahalia
made the church rock,
made the church holler,
made the church say,

A-
men!

Bill Harris is the author of numerous plays that have received more than fifty productions throughout the country. They include *Stories about the Old Days, Every Goodbye Ain't Gone, Robert Johnson: Trick the Devil,* and *Riffs.*

Harris is an Associate Professor of English at Wayne State University in Detroit. He was formerly Production Coordinator for the Jazzmobile and the New Federal Theatre in New York, as well as Chief Curator at Detroit's Museum of African American History. His plays have been published in **The National Black Drama Anthology**; **New Plays for the Black Theatre, Voices of Color** edited by Woodie King, Jr., and **African American Literature** edited by Al Young.